I0438264

# Heaven, Hell and Beyond:

## *The Divine Encounters of One European Family*

## Val & Mariya Kanchelov

### Special Contribution From Yoel Kanchelov

*We dedicate this book to our
precious sons, Yoel and Raphael.
We are fully convinced that through
the grace of the Lord Jesus Christ,
you will be shaped into fearless knights
of His Cross, carrying the Good News
of The Kingdom even farther than we
will ever be able to reach.*

# Table of Contents

# Introduction

A. About the Book

The purpose of this book is not merely to attract your attention to the supernatural side of life. As we explore the different dimensions of the spiritual realm (Heaven, hell, angelic and demonic presence, etc.) from various perspectives, and through the experiences of a few different individuals, we would like also to give you hope, to sharpen your expectation for the coming kingdom of the Lord Jesus Christ, and to help with your preparation for it. John the Baptist, the forerunner of the King, made the following statement regarding the nature of the ministry he was entrusted with:

*"The voice of one crying in the wilderness: Prepare the way of the Lord;*
*Make His paths straight.*
*Every valley shall be filled*
*And every mountain and hill brought low;*
*The crooked places shall be made straight*
*And the rough ways smooth;*
*And all flesh shall see the salvation of God."*

Luke 3:4-6

In the ancient world when a king would visit a certain place, preparations were made to accommodate him and make his visit more delightful. In the same manner, the Holy Spirit commands us through the voice of John the Baptist to forsake our evil ways and to start walking in the ways of righteousness. Notice that this text emphasizes our responsibility in preparing the Earth for the King Jesus. We have to repent before the Lord (confess our sin and change our way of thinking) and to commit to a new devotion to Him (Revelation 3:18).

Also, we have to realize that the world as we know it has come to the end; a new era (not the one from the "new age" teachings) is about to begin. The Holy Spirit tells us that the mountains and hills (symbols of the various kinds of human government) will dissolve in order for the King Jesus to regain the complete reign over the whole Earth and to be "All in all." Simply stated, the Good News of the Kingdom is: "God reigns and His Kingdom is about to be restored on the Earth!" This is the real Gospel that was committed to the Apostles and was preached and demonstrated in the Early Church. Then, distractions from the primary message and heresies came in, the truth was watered-down and the Church's witness became weak. God, in His Mercy, started restoring the truth to His body – one ray of light at a time (Isaiah 28:10) because that was the maximum intensity of light humanity could handle.

After the Reformation, Christians in every generation, looking at each new ray of light that the Spirit of Jehovah was revealing to them, thought they had the complete truth while they experienced just glimpses of it. Righteousness through faith, salvation from sin, baptism in the Holy Spirit, healing of the body, victory over the flesh and the world, to mention only a few, as precious as they are, are still just a part of God's greater purpose, which is <u>the restoration of His Kingdom on the Earth</u>. We have allowed important but lesser truths to distract us from the ultimate Good News. Because of the trees, we have not been able to see the forest.

But thank God! Christians all over the world are returning to the basics and starting to preach the Good News of the Kingdom and to demonstrate its restoring power which can reverse any curse mankind has brought upon itself through its disobedience to the King.

## B. The Nature of Visions and Dreams

We do not believe that visions and dreams are given to establish a new doctrine or revelation, but to enlighten an existing one. Our belief is that all the spiritual revelation humanity needs could be found in the pages of the Bible and is administrated to us by the Holy Spirit as we seek Him. We completely reject any doctrines or revelations that contradict the written Word of God (Psalm 119:89). Jesus is the Truth and the Holy Spirit is the Revealer of the Truth (Jesus).

The message in this book requires your personal discernment in the same way your reaction (acceptation or rejection) to Jesus as Savior and Lord requires the same discernment. The message is as radical as it could possibly be. If you are looking for a watered-down, politically correct or socially acceptable Christianity, you may want to stop reading right now.

The fact that the Lord in His mercy has chosen to give this message through us, does not make us more spiritual or mature than anybody else, but rather reveals His gracious and loving nature, and His ability to use the weak and foolish things of this world (1 Corinthians 1: 27). Probably the only two characteristics of true spirituality are love and humility. The revelations we received do not make us immune to sin and mistakes. History shows that the torch of the glorious Gospel has been carried by real flesh-and-blood individuals who have had their share of failures. As someone once said, Christianity is a perfect life to be lived by imperfect individuals.

Finally, we are looking at the message in this book as a gracious (and probably final for some) invitation to the people without Jesus to come to know Him, and His children to make an even more radical commitment to the Kingdom.

# I Saw The Heaven Open...

## Atlanta, Georgia

**Mariya**: It was in the late afternoon of January 6, 2009. As I and my husband Val were praying in the Spirit, suddenly the Heaven was open. I saw the throne of God, and the One sitting on it had His face covered by a cloud. Behind His head there were three stars which formed a triangle. Then I saw another person in front of the throne. At first I thought it was Jesus, but almost immediately I was given the understanding that it was Michael, the archangel. He was worshiping the Father and was listening carefully to His commands. The Father was talking in a language that sounded much like Hebrew. Then I saw Michael on a black horse. The horse looked like one of the horses the knights used in medieval times in Europe. It was fully armored for battle. Behind Michael there was a huge army of angels, almost like a sea. I was given supernatural understanding of what the Father was saying. I understood that we were right before the last battle of this age. The Father instructed Michael to divide his armies into four formations. On one side, the Father told him, to put those who

He would send to fight for the backslidden, for their return to the faith. Another unit was formed in order to go and fight for the salvation of the souls who do not yet know the Lord. A third formation was separated to fight for those who are a part of the Church but still are in bondage to evil powers. The fourth formation was the biggest one. Those angels were given assignment to fight for those who walk in the Light and who had their lamps lit.

As I was watching, the Word of the Lord came to me:

*Thus says the Spirit of the Lord to all of you who pray and believe. Light your lamps. Clean your clothes. Gird yourselves and prepare for the last battle. Because it will be like in Egypt when gross darkness fell upon the Egyptians and there was light upon My people. It is the same way in the spiritual world right now. Not only My blood but My light is upon you. And if you keep it by faith, if you keep it by constant prayer, if you keep your candles lit, I will be able to conquer for you, I will be able to lead you in triumphant procession and make you a part of the army which fights for the backslidden and those who are still to be added to the Book of Life. I separated you for the time you live in, I foresaw these days and gave you special abilities so you could endure. The hard days will be for the unbelievers, but blessing, glory and honor will be for these who seek Me daily and trust in Me. Time is coming when I will send Michael and he will fight personally for you who believe and trust in Me, who live where the throne of Satan is* (from my understanding, the Holy Spirit was referring to the United States)*, whose names are special to Me, whose names belong to the ones walking in glory, not to the fearful but to the ones conquering evil by good. Your life is in My hands. Do not be afraid of death because I have conquered it. If death could overcome you, you would have been dead already. But I conquered the evil one and I am conquering him every day. Trust in Me, speak according to your faith, according to your vision, according to My Word. Be consistent. I am with you through all these days. Not a single hair will fall from your head because I have sworn to My name to protect you, and I will use you for My work.*

The Spirit of the Lord continued to talk to us, mostly about our home and ministry. At a certain point, He again made a reference to the United States of America:

*I saw this place to be Sodom and Gomorrah, but because of you* (the people who pray and believe) *I will spare what I can spare and I will rescue what I can rescue.*

Now, do not misunderstand us. We deeply love and care about the United States of America, but apparently the stench of her sin has reached the nostrils of God. We do not know if this nation has reached the point of no return. What we know is even if this is the case, God still can preserve from the midst of her those who trust and believe in Him.

I had a similar vision of the throne of God about twenty years ago (you can read about it in one of the next chapters). One of the main differences in the current vision was in the multitude of the angels who were preparing for the battle. My husband believes this vision refers (as far as timing is concerned) to the part of John's vision described in the Book of Revelation, 12:7, and it is an indication about the place we are in God's timetable – right before the tribulation, which precedes the coming of Christ's Kingdom. Even if he is not one hundred percent correct, the message is that <u>it is almost midnight on the spiritual and historical clock of humanity and our Master is at the door</u>! Be ready!!!

# The Chapter of Beginnings

A. Mariya's Perspective

Growing up in communist Bulgaria, I was able to see different dimensions of the spiritual world. Beside the dark demonic ruler controlling the government, I have witnessed various manifestations of the evil power on a more personal level. For example, during one of the visits to my grandmother who practiced witchcraft, I observed the following phenomenon: Our whole family was gathered in one of the rooms when we heard noise from the room next door where nobody stayed. We checked to see where the noise was coming from, but there was no one, only the table, which had been a mess, now was set and completely prepared. Our blood froze from terror. On another instance, in the same building, a demonic spirit in bodily form appeared to my uncle and scared him almost to death.

Next to my grandmother's involvement with the occult, the divorce of my parents opened another demonic gate of influence in my life. My father's disregard to the marriage covenant released a spiritual force even greater than the emotional devastation that took place. At the age of eight, I found myself full of rebellion and hatred, and my body was so weak that in the following years I developed many different diseases – asthma, anemia, leukemia, etc. Sometimes these diseases escalated to the point where my doctors expected a fatal ending. But God, in His mercy, had another plan. He used one of those incidents to change my destiny forever.

During one of the emergency visits to the hospital, the doctors gave my mother the following report: "We cannot do anything more to save your daughter. You'd better start making preparations for her funeral." These are the worst words a mother can hear. My mom was in despair. Sometimes desperation is not a bad place to start. It is simply a realization that so far you have applied wrong principles or have made wrong choices. In what seemed to be her darkest hour, my mom made a commitment which would shape the eternal destiny of the generations after her. Mom realized that all the help available on Earth was not enough and she turned her eyes upon Heaven. In a way similar to how the childless Hanna received Samuel from the Lord (1 Samuel 1, 2), she made the following vow before the Lord: "God, if you save the life of my daughter, I will give her back to You." I believe that was the point where my life began to change.

Shortly after that, the doctors reexamined me and found that my condition slowly but steadily was improving. But even a greater change was to come. A few years later during my high school study, a classmate of mine shared the Good News of Jesus' death, burial and resurrection with me. The King's love was so compelling to me that I could do nothing but give my life to Him Who carried my sin on the cross. The greatest adventure in my life was about to begin....

A few years later, while coming down the church aisle in response to the altar call, the Holy Spirit would remind my mom about that fateful day when she vowed my life to Him and she would uncontrollably burst into tears.

## B. Val's Perspective

It was the autumn of 1989, and as I walked the distance between gorgeous downtown Sofia, the capital of Bulgaria, and the place where I stayed, heavy thoughts occupied my mind. I was not able to enjoy either the clear sky or the awesome architecture of the buildings lightened by the street lights. I was a student at the best law school in my country, with a promising career in front of me, dating a very intelligent and beautiful young lady, having parents who loved me and supported me, but something was missing. I felt as empty inside as anyone could feel. I had tried everything to get rid of those feelings of emptiness and hopelessness: I went to parties, used alcohol, tried some eastern religions, immersed myself in the arts, etc. Unfortunately, I had not seen any improvement. On the contrary, things had become even worse.

In addition, circumstances were changing around me. The communist government collapsed and the country seemed to be on the road to democracy, but nothing seemed to be changing on the inside of me. My loneliness and dissatisfaction with life were becoming greater and greater.

Little did I expect that very soon God would intervene and capture my life in such a way that I would never be able (nor willing) to escape from His grip. But God's plan for my life was set in motion.

During our next summer break, I and a few friends of mine went to the Black Sea, to a small town called Achtopol. We were preparing for a vacation and getting ready to do any wild thing college students could do. I did not know I was about to have one of those so-called "meetings with destiny." It came in a form of a few young people singing songs about Jesus and talking about God's love. The first night I spoke with them I argued fiercely and even thought I won the debate. These young people were mature enough to ignore my foolishness and invited me to a church service on the following day. I and my friends had nothing else to do and decided to accept the invitation. The service took place in the open summer theater. Sitting on the wooden benches we could see both the stage with the preacher and the gorgeous sunset over the sea. I will never forget that evening. I do not recall much of the preaching but was really impressed when that group of Christians prayed for a mute boy and suddenly his speech was restored. Later I discovered that healing of the sick is one of the signs following the preaching of the Word of God (Mark 16:18).

At that point I stopped looking at the stage and started gazing at the sea horizon and asking questions to the invisible and unknown God who obviously was trying to communicate His love to me. I had done some study into the different Eastern religions and, although I knew it would be in vain, I started asking the different so-called "gods" and "teachers" if they were real and who was the unknown person that was reaching out to me. Of course, I received no answer. Then, after skipping a few of them, I went straight to Jesus Christ. I asked Him a simple question: "Jesus, are you God?" Immediately, something like a beam of light came into my spirit and I knew without a shadow of a doubt that I did not have to search anymore. That light was invisible for the human eye, but was so real that I could see it everywhere: over me, over the theater, over the sea…. Later, I discovered in the Bible that was the light that enlightens every man coming into this world (Gospel of John 1:9). This was the light that confronted the self-righteous Saul on his way to Damascus (Acts 9) and transformed him into the humble Paul, the Apostle. None of my friends who were in that meeting received it. They were continuing with the same cynical attitude. But I knew something had happened: a new life had begun inside of me right there, in the town of Achtopol.

Little did I know that seven years later I would come back to that small town, but this time married to Mariya, for our honeymoon trip.

## C. Yoel's Perspective

I will start where my Dad left off – on the seashore, not on the Black Sea but on the Baltic Sea. I was born in Kiel, Germany, in a clinic located on the shore. My parents stayed in Kiel only a short time after my birth and that's why I have no memories of my birthplace. When Mom and Dad talk about Kiel, they usually mention God's faithfulness. It was a very difficult time for them, but they knew God was still in control of their destiny. Years before they even thought about coming to Kiel, the Holy Spirit gave them some dreams which they did not understand at that time. For instance, my mother had seen in a dream that one of the OB nurses during the delivery of her baby was named Anna. She forgot about it, but then in the midst of the painful birth (which was only a part of the difficulties my parents faced) she saw the name tag on one of the nurses, and, you already guessed – it said Anna. The name "Anna" means "grace" and just that reminder was an injection of hope into Mom's heart, and she was assured that God's grace was abundant toward her. God's grace is everything you need, too.

Three years after my birth, in 2001, we moved to the United States, where not long after that I came to know the Lord Jesus Christ. And this is everything I am going to say for now....

# Heaven

A. Heavenly Calling

**Mariya**: It happened shortly after I gave my life to the Lord and became a part of a church who believed in the power of prayer. It was the spring of 1989. On that particular Saturday afternoon I attended a small group where we prayed for a few hours. It was already dark when I and a friend of mine decided to go home. It was a beautiful night with a clear sky. We were walking and still praying when we noticed that there was only one cloud in the sky. As we came to my apartment, the cloud approached us and became bigger and bigger. Then the cloud took the shape of a hand pointing to a certain direction.

We laughed at it and continued our walk. But the cloud kept getting closer and closer. A few minutes later, it took the form of a cross. Then it became a dove. Suddenly, the presence of God and holy fear came upon us and we could hardly move. Looking at the sky, we saw a royal throne and a Person looking like a man sitting on it. A cloud covered His face and behind His head there were three stars forming a triangle. His hair was white, implying He was the

Ancient of Days (Daniel 7:13) who had the wisdom of the ages. Then He lifted His hand and we saw a sickle in it. He said: *"Go and tell my church that the harvest is plentiful but the laborers are few. I am coming very soon to gather the wheat in My storehouse and to burn the chaff with fire."* Then everything disappeared like a vapor.

The presence of God was still heavy on us. We looked around thinking that the Rapture might be taking place. The strangest thing was that there was nobody on that particular street which usually had a lot of traffic in the evenings. Then we started running toward my place deeply shaken by what we saw and heard.

B. My Visit to Heaven

**Mariya**: Everything started as a dream. I was dreaming that I was together with other people from our church, when suddenly I heard a trumpet voice saying: "Separate Mariya for the work to which I have called her." Then an angel clothed in light appeared in my room and took me by the hand. My spirit left my body and exited the room through the window that was open (it was the late part of the spring of 1989, and I kept that window open at night). The angel took me through what looked like a great shield of light and we arrived in the center of what I knew was the Heavenly Jerusalem. I saw the dwelling place of God and the river of life coming out of it. Then I saw what I recognized to be the tree of life. It looked like the river of life was going through its roots. I heard noise to my side, and when I turned, I saw a group of children with flowers, balls and balloons that they were throwing in the air. As they were doing that, they were shouting: "Hosanna to the Son of David!" Later I learned those were children who had been aborted or had premature deaths.

The next thing that captured my attention were the streets. They were made of gold and you could see through them. I could not help to notice all the people who were walking up and down the streets. Apparently they were engaged in various works and activities, but they were not stressed or preoccupied. Nobody was just flying around on clouds like some religious preconceptions suggest.

Suddenly, the angel who had been with me disappeared. I turned around and saw that a man approached me. He was wearing a leather cloth with a golden girdle around his waist. My first thought was that he was Jesus but he interrupted my thoughts, saying: "Mariya, I am not Jesus. I am John the Baptist." He continued: "The Father, the Son and the Holy Spirit are having a meeting and that is the reason Jesus did not come to meet you personally." He pointed to the dwelling where the Trinity was having their meeting. I saw two angels (or cherubs) with swords in their hands standing in front of the building. From time to time they would cross their swords and light would come from them to the Earth. I asked John the Baptist what that was. He answered that they were the answers to saints' prayers. Then he turned back to me again and said: "I do not have much time to talk to you about other things because you have a strictly determined time by God to stay here. I am the one who talks to you because what you have to do on the Earth is what I was doing. Tell the people that the Kingdom of God is coming and they have to prepare themselves. By your ministry, God will turn "the hearts of the children to the fathers and the hearts of the fathers to the children and the disobedient to the wisdom of the just."

After saying all this, he departed from me and the angel who transported me earlier returned. The angel said: "It is time for you to go back. If you stay longer, your return will be difficult." I did not want to go back. As I was gazing at the various homes and buildings, I asked the angel which was my home. He answered shortly that the location of your house is based on the reward for the work you have done on the Earth: the greater the reward was, the closer the location will be to the dwelling place of God.

Then I felt like my spirit was sucked by some kind of extra powerful vacuum and the next thing I know is that I was back in my body. I saw the concerned face of my mother leaning over me while she was checking my temperature, which was low. Obviously, when the spirit leaves the human body, the body immediately starts to decay (James 2:26).

My mother decided not to send me to school on that day and I had opportunity to restore physically after my journey and to meditate on the calling I had just received. I do not believe I am the only person with a call like that. I know about other people who have received the same calling or have had similar experiences. We can clearly see in the Bible that the mantles of certain prophets/preachers have been transferred to other people throughout history. Sometimes the mantle of one person has been carried by many people in different generations. For instance, the anointing that was on Elijah came on Elisha, on John the Baptist, on parts of the Church today, on at least one of the witnesses in the Book of Revelation. Unfortunately, there have been people even in the most recent history of the Church, who because of the powerful manifestations of the Spirit in their ministries, assumed they were Elijah. They erred because they did not realize the difference between the anointing (the power to serve) and the personality. You may receive somebody else's anointing (as the Holy Spirit wills) but you will never receive someone's personality.

According to the calling I received, I have tried my best to serve God with this anointing. Shortly after my visit to Heaven, I had the privilege to be a part of the revival that took place in Bulgaria in the early Nineties. Since then I have served various individuals, churches and groups, and am always amazed at the faithfulness and the power of our Lord Jesus.

## C. Yoel's Glimpse Into Heaven

**Val**: One of the concerns I had when Yoel was still a toddler was how I would prevent him from craving and yielding to all the distractions, the occult and immorality that attacked the younger generation from every side. We were doing our part of natural things to keep him away from all that pollution, but we knew it would take more than a system of dos and don'ts to compete with it. In the beginning of 2005, I had a dream in which God showed me He would attract Yoel to Himself by letting him experience the reality of His Divine presence. Later on that year, our whole family visited Bulgaria, where Mariya and I preached at a certain conference. The morning after the conference, we were scheduled to travel on a few days vacation to the Black Sea. I saw that Yoel, who was seven at that time, was sleeping unusually deep and tried to wake him without success. I continued with my preparation, and later on, he woke up. We departed from Sofia and were on our way to the sea when he said: "Mom, Dad, listen. When I was asleep this morning, God took me to Heaven!" That surely grabbed our attention. We asked him how he knew it was Heaven. With the limited vocabulary of a seven-year-old, he said something like: "There was no sickness and problems, only peace." We asked him if he saw anybody. Yoel replied: "Yes, I saw Jesus. He hugged me and told me that He loved me." That was everything he could remember (and probably everything a seven-year-old could grasp) but it was so significant to me. I knew God was fulfilling His promise to attract Yoel to Himself. What I did not know was this was just the beginning of the divine encounters in Yoel's life, which together with the Word and our prayers would start shaping Yoel's journey of faith.

"**I love you**." This is the deepest message you could receive from Jesus. You don't even have to hear it in a supernatural experience. It is all over the pages of the Bible. Take a moment and meditate on the Word that says:

*"For God so loved the world that he gave His only begotten Son that whoever believes in Him should not perish but have everlasting life."*

John 3:16

# Earth: Spiritual Warfare
# And Divine Encounters

A. Spiritual Warfare

**Mariya**: Ever since my new birth, I have been intensely involved in spiritual warfare. In fact, I realized the spiritual nature of many of the problems and situations I had been dealing with. It became clear to me that even some of the diseases against my body had spiritual causes. One such problem was the asthma I had suffered for many years. The minute I received the baptism in the Holy Ghost, the spirit which caused the asthma left and for the last twenty years I have never had another symptom. I am not advocating that all sickness and infirmities are caused by direct demonic influence, but Jesus Himself said some were (Luke 13:10-16).

Another trial I had in my physical body was when the doctors found that the anemia I had had for years developed into leukemia. At that time there was no reliable treatment for it, and once again, I was sentenced to death. I became extremely weak, but this time I had the comfort that if I died I would go and be in the glorious presence of the Lord.

But again, God intervened on my behalf. The Holy Spirit put in the hearts of some people in my church to fast for three days and pray for my recovery. Shortly after that, I was examined again by a doctor who pretended to be an atheist. After seeing the test results (which indicated almost complete recovery), she told my Mom: "Please take your daughter and her paperwork and leave before I forsake my atheism and start believing in God." My life was spared again!

On other occasions the satanic assault was not even disguised in a form of sickness or something seemingly natural. I remember one evening not very long after I became a Christian, I was going home and was close to my place when somebody approached me in the dark alley. I turned around and saw a person looking like a man, having a pale face with unnatural beauty. He was wearing something like a black robe and a big black hat, almost like sombrero. He said: "You had a covenant with me and you belong to me!" I did not even have time to get afraid. Suddenly, holy boldness arose inside of me and I shouted at him:" I have been redeemed by the blood of Jesus! I belong to Jesus! Now, get lost!" The dark character disappeared immediately.

Later on, while thinking about what had happened, I remember that my uncle described almost the same encounter, apparently with the same being. Also, I came to realize that the satanic covenant he was talking about must have come into existence through some of my grandmother's occult practices. But thank God for the blood of Jesus! Thank God for the blood of the New Covenant, which has made us free so that "being delivered from the hands of our enemies, we might serve Him without fear in holiness and righteousness before Him all the days of our life" (Luke 1:74-75).

B. Divine And Angelic Encounters

**Mariya**: 1996 was a year of a very intense spiritual warfare. The former Communist Party had regained the political power in Bulgaria and was trying to impose all kinds of restrictions on the new evangelical churches. The year before, God instructed me and some friends of mine to move to the United States. While waiting on God to open the door for us, I got actively engaged in intercession for our nation, the Body of Christ, and unsaved people all over the world. At that time I was living with a friend and had the tremendous privilege to have her as a prayer partner. For a period of less than six months, we had at least two divine encounters.

The first one happened on June 26. We were fasting and praying for the Word that had been sown by the Church in the hearts of men to produce and return to God with mature fruit. While we were in prayer, God sent two angels to strengthen us. In their hands they had some kind of containers with some liquid that they poured over us. The angels explained that was the pain of God about the people who are not saved yet. One of the angels said:

*"You will be like these people. The bones in your bodies will be weakened because of the heaviness of sin which will be over you. You will be like separated from God with no way of escape. Only we will be here to strengthen you and to make your fast successful. But on the third day, you will have victory. God's power will return on you in the way it came on Jesus*

*when He rose from the dead."* The angel continued: *"We will put your words in the containers and take them back to God and in such way they* (our words) *will succeed in accomplishing God's work on the Earth."*

The angel assigned to my friend, who was an anointed musician, told her:

*"You must start every day with praise."* Then he touched her mouth and continued: *"The praise will refresh you during the fast and will open the way for God to move on your behalf."*

My angel told me to use the knowledge I had about fasting and to write down everything that would happen during these three days. One of the results that I saw in the days after the fast had a very personal meaning to me. Less than two weeks later, my brother gave his life to Jesus! And if you have not done it yet yourself, don't delay another moment: repent of your sins, ask Jesus to cleanse you through His blood and invite Him into your heart. May God bless you!

Later that same year I and my friend had another encounter different in form but still related to the prayer on behalf of the unsaved (in that case interceding that the wrath of God be turned away from our nation). That particular morning I had a dream in which disastrous rain and snow caused a big flood. In the dream I asked: *"Lord, what can we do now, when the disaster has already come?"* Then a book was opened up in front of me and I saw written with beautiful letters: **Psalm 22** and **1996** (which was the year that that was happening). After that I heard a voice which told me: "*I have said it in Psalm 22.*"

The dream was over but I still did not understand its meaning. Later, I realized that God was urging us to another fast, Psalm 22 also named **The Suffering, Praise** and **Posterity of Messiah,** and which contains the three basics stages of intercessory prayer: **The suffering** is your identification with the people on whose behalf you intercede**; Praise** is your acknowledgment of the righteousness and justice of God; **Posterity** is the final product of your prayer.

But our day was not over yet. Around three p.m., as we were praying and confessing our sins, we found ourselves in the throne room of God in Heaven. We saw the Father looking at the books of our lives and with the blood from the altar He was erasing the sins we were confessing (He was covering what was written with the blood and it was disappearing). Then we saw Gabriel, the archangel who said: "*I look at His face every day. You are standing before the One who a bruised reed will not break and smoking flax will not quench. Worship Him because you are in His temple*". As we prostrated ourselves before the Father, another voice, which we recognized belonged to Jesus, said: "*Say: We are servants of The Almighty God, Possessor of Heaven and Earth, whose authority is over every Earthly authority.*" Then He continued: "*You will glorify My name; you will go everywhere I am sending you and will proclaim My Word. With My Name, you will open every closed door in front of you. I am expecting soon your sacrifice* (another fast and intercession) *with which you will turn the wrath of the Father away from your country. And the anointing which is on you will soften the hearts of the people I am sending you to."*

Then the Father told me:*" Your name won't be any longer <u>Anna Mariya</u> but <u>Mariya Esther</u>."* That was not a mere suggestion but a command from The Lord of the Armies. Before we left the heavenly temple, Gabriel took a fiery coal from the altar, gave it to us and said: *"Eat and be purified. Eat from the Word; be strengthened in your faith and go! With labor you will accomplish God's desire on the Earth."*

After that we were back in the room. Our hearts were burning with desire to go and conquer for the glory of the King! And sure enough, the fast and prayer turned God's wrath and the country was spared at least for that period of time.

# Coming Down From His Throne

**Val**: How important are you to the King? What is your worth in His Kingdom? Is your significance enough for Him to set aside for a moment the rule and management over the entire Universe with its complexity and sophistication beyond human imagination and to fulfill some desire of yours? Is a need of yours so important to the Royalty that He would step from His throne and visit you with the solution? The Bible says "yes" to your importance and value in the sight of God over and over again. King David's exclamation is recorded in Psalm 8: 4-6:

*"What is man that you are mindful of him?*
*And the son of man that you visited him?*
*For you have made him a little lower than Elohim,*
*And you have crowned him with glory and honor.*
*You have made him to have dominion over the works*
*of Your hands;*
*You have put all things under his feet..."*

The Lord Jesus Himself emphasized many times the value of the human soul in His Father's eyes and at the end offered His own blood as the currency worthy to redeem our degenerated and sinful lives (John 3:16).

You are priceless in His sight! Not because you have done something special to deserve it, but because The King chose to count you priceless. That is the reason you can expect His goodness to manifest in your life as He responds to your prayer. Now, let's go back to the place Mariya left off…

Shortly after the events she described in the previous chapter, both she and I received invitations to preach at a conference hold in the church of a common friend of ours. We were not married nor engaged at that time. Five years before that event God told me that she would be my wife and I, disregarding God's timing, went to Mariya to share my feelings for her. The day before I approached her, the Holy Spirit told her: "Regardless of whomever proposes to you, your answer should be 'No'." Marriage was the last thing on her mind at that time and that's why she was surprised by the instruction. You might have already guessed: the conversation we had on the following day was disastrous to me. I left thinking I had missed God this time and also my feelings were severely hurt. Many years later I realized that God spared us from combining immaturity and strong characters (both of us were 21 years old at that time) and creating a marriage that would probably not last a few months. However, I was feeling at the lowest point of my life. I loved Mariya and knew that she was the most unique person I had ever met and I would ever meet. But I loved God even more. Regardless of the emotional setback, I decided to pursue God's presence even more. Jesus pointed to the cost of discipleship and stated that no human relationship should stand in its way (Mathew 10:37-39). I knew very well the story of how Abraham was ready to sacrifice Isaac and how God restored that relationship and used it for a much higher purpose. I decided to apply the principle behind the story and submitted everything to God, believing He was still in control. With everything on the altar, I decided to apply another principle from God's Word. The Bible says in Mathew 6:33 that if we seek first the Kingdom of God, everything else (which includes marriage in God's will) will be added unto you.

That is the nature of the covenant: if you are fully dedicated to Him, you will be able to experience His perfect commitment of provision, too. So I decided to look not for God's permissive but perfect will in the area of marriage. Along the way I was tempted to change my focus in this area, but He was faithful to sustain my commitment with His power.

I know that many Christians, including ministers, believe that you can marry anybody as long as he or she is in the faith and meets certain moral require-ments, and you just choose between many persons. I am not here to argue with such points of view, but please consider the following example: you are called to a political career in Washington, D.C. and the person you want to marry feels that God called him/her as a missionary to Mozambique. Even if that marriage would work, none of the partners would function in the fullness of God's calling and, since our most important purpose should be to fulfill His will on this Earth, they will fail, fully or partially.

I believe God has chosen a unique person to stand next to you and to help you to become the history maker He has called you to be. In case the person prepared for you fails to walk in His path, He would come with plans B, C, and D, etc. until He gets you settled. His faithfulness is awesome! And in case you feel that you missed God's will in this area consider His forgiving and restoring grace. He is more than able to create a beauty of your mess!

Remember King David from the Bible? He violated both God's and man's law for a short gratification with Bathsheba, and he had to pay horrible consequences for that. But in the midst of that whole mess, he decided to run to God and not from Him. He was able to appropriate God's redeeming grace, and Bathsheba, a woman that should had never married David, became a part of the Royal genealogy of Messiah (2 Samuel 11,12). If God did it for David, He will do it for you, too.

But let me go back to that church conference, which took place in the month of February 1997. The blessing of God was on those meetings. Besides the rich Word, some remarkable healings occurred as a result of our prayers. At the end of the conference, right before our departure, the hosting pastor and his family, the speakers and at least one more person were in his apartment ready to pray for safe trip on our way home. What we thought would be a quick prayer turned into a much longer spiritual experience. The presence of God filled the room. The Holy Spirit started manifesting Himself through several of the so-called "spiritual gifts" (1 Corinthians 12).

The strangest thing was that everything was happening in an atmosphere with various distractions. To mention just two: that pastor's son who was between two and three years old had to use his potty and needed some assistance with that; his grandmother who was not very friendly to Christianity at that time was creating a slight commotion from the room next door. However, none of that could prevent God from manifesting His presence during that prayer.

Our physical bodies could hardly bear it. We had had experiences with a heavy anointing prior to that, but this time it was different. There was a Person in the room. I knew without a shadow of a doubt that it was the Lord Jesus Himself!

While I had overwhelming knowledge of Jesus' presence without seeing Him, God opened the spiritual eyes of some of the other people, and they were able to see the King. He gave us some general directions for the Church in Bulgaria and also for everyone's ministry and personal life.

As far as my ministry was concerned, after applying His instructions during the following months, I was able to reach a few thousand people in a nation pretty hostile to the Gospel at that particular point and see, in my opinion, a significant harvest. Speaking about my personal life, one of the things Jesus said was: *"Soon I will bless you in a way I have never blessed you before."*

In the weeks following that glorious experience, I would meditate daily upon every word He told me that day. I would see these things coming to pass one by one. But I could not understand what He meant by the aforementioned promise. I would try to compare and find place for it in different areas of my life, but the puzzle remained incomplete. I knew that if I lacked wisdom and asked for it, God would give it to me without reproach (James 1:5). And surely He did. He used one of His ministers (a woman whose integrity and ministry I personally knew and esteemed highly).

In May of the same year I received a call from her and she told me God gave her a word for me but she was led to speak it to me in person. Since I knew how precise she was in the ministry, I agreed to travel to her city and meet her. After we met and prayed, she delivered God's word to me.

The following words were a part of God's instruction for me:

*"For the last few years, God has been preparing, building and polishing you not only for the ministry, but also for your personal life. You have buried your desire for marriage, but now is the time for Me to resurrect it. If you let Me do it, you won't experience any limitations in your ministry…The woman I have prepared for you is a servant, who by her intercession will keep Satan away from you. With her prayers she will raise walls of fire around you. She will be for your protection, support and inspiration. She is precious in My sight because of her purity and love. Now is the time I want to bless you. Enter into this area and into My joy. Because I have never put*

*you to shame and I am the Lord who deals with you wonderfully...."*

I do not have to say that I was thrilled with the news. Also, I had the witness in my spirit this was a genuine word from Heaven; even more the lady who delivered the message knew almost nothing about my personal life. But a question still remained: Who was the person the Holy Spirit was referring to as my future wife? God even told me He had already testified to her but who was her? Another concern I had was that I would never marry somebody I do not love with my whole heart or who had a different vision than me. After spending more hours in meditation, prayer and counseling, I came to realize that only one person had all the characteristics the Spirit of God was talking about. That was Mariya, the girl who rejected my approach five years prior to that, the girl who I had never stopped loving with all my heart. I was given a second chance, and I fully intended not to waste it.

I will never forget that sunny June day and that café in one of the most beautiful parts of Sofia when she said, "Yes" to my proposal. Later on, she confirmed that the same Holy Spirit who five years prior told her "Whoever comes to you with a marriage proposal, reject it" now witnessed to her about me and about the right timing.

Why am I sharing such a personal story? Certainly, not to brag how spiritual I am or to say that you must have a similar experience in order for your marriage to work. While fully convinced that you have to discern spiritually God's will for your marriage, I am not advocating that you should seek some kind of spectacular experience similar to what happened to us. God, in His sovereignty, decided to deal with us in this way. Neither am I advocating that if God started the journey, it would be a smooth journey, or even successful. Marriage is a daily hard work. Even if God started it, every day you still have to make dozens, probably hundreds of decisions that affect directly or indirectly your spouse or children. What I want to do is to brag on King Jesus' faithfulness and reliability.

Also, I would like to provoke you to a new devotion in your walk with Him. Go beyond your previous limits. Don't be afraid to trust the Lord even with what is most sacred to your heart. He will never let you down! You are His beloved. Seek first His Kingdom and His righteousness and everything else will be added unto you. The King will find a way to communicate His wisdom (what to do) to you. Even if He himself has to leave His throne and deliver it in person to you like He did for us! I will say it again, trust Him!

# Hell: A Ten-Year-Old's Journey to the Center of the Earth

**Val**: John the Baptist prophesied about the twofold mission of Jesus: to baptize with the Holy Spirit and to baptize with fire. Baptism with the Spirit ultimately means unlimited access and immersion into the Kingdom of Heaven (Romans 14:17). That part of the mission Jesus has already fulfilled. The Kingdom is open to everyone who believes in the King's amnesty for his/her transgressions and humbles himself/herself by repentance. The second part of Jesus' mandate (the baptism with fire) is still to be fulfilled. Fire implies judgment. Both believers and unbelievers will go through a fiery judgment but there will be a difference in the very nature of that judgment.

Believers' judgment is not for determination of whether or not we will spend eternity with God. That case was closed when we accepted Jesus as our Lord and Savior (Romans 8:1). The judgment through fire is to determine what kind of reward the believer will receive for his/her deeds, if any (1 Corinthians 3:12-15).

The case with the fire that will come upon unbelievers is different. John the Baptist said about Jesus that *"He will burn the chaff* (the people who reject His sacrifice and mercy) *with fire* (Luke 3:17). Jesus Himself spoke about the fire that will test everyone (Mark 9:49) and John the Apostle specified a few categories of people whose eternal destiny will be in the lake of fire (Revelation 21:8). Fire is inevitable; the question is which of the aforementioned two judgments you will participate in.

In the current chapter Yoel shares an experience that would mark his and others' lives forever. At the beginning of May 2008, I had a very strange dream: In my dream I saw Yoel going to hell and the strangest thing was that I was not terrified. When I woke up, I thought about it but still had no clue about its meaning or interpretation. I knew that Yoel had given his life to the Lord at an early age and even with him having need of correction in different ways, I did not think he was on the way to damnation. Especially not at his tender age – he was ten years old at that time. Something did not fit well in the whole picture.

A few weeks later I received a call at work from my wife. I knew that something was going on because of the vibration of her voice. She said: "Yoel told me that last night God took him and showed him hell." She started describing what Yoel had already shared with her. I interrupted her: "Please put him on the phone!" I wanted to make sure the dream was not merely a product of his imagination or the result of an upset stomach. I knew the character of my son and his lack of interest in religious speculations but still wanted to verify if the experience he had had was genuine.

After a short examination over the phone, I told him: "Write down everything you saw. I do not want you to forget it." Yoel replied: "Dad, how could I ever forget all these screams?" I felt inconsiderate.

When you read his testimony, please take into account the fact that an observation of the same subject from a ten-year-old most likely will be different from an observation of a forty- or even a twenty-year-old; not that much in substance but in focus and details. Also, the intensity that a ten-year-old can carry and describe is lesser in its extent. Still, the Spirit of God promised in Acts 2:17 that in these last days, the young people, "Shall prophesy and <u>see visions</u>...."

Visions and dreams are given not to replace or even to back up God's Word but to attract people to its truth. And the truth of the Word is that hell is real; it exists right now; it was created for Satan and his angels, but the humans who refuse to give up on sin will end up there. Jesus provided a living way of escape through His sacrifice. Call on His name and you shall be saved (Romans 10:13).

**Yoel**: I would like to start saying I do not know if the story you are about to read is a result of an out-of-body experience or a vision of hell. All I know is that it was real and one of the reasons Jesus showed it to me is to warn you not to go there. It is a terrible place of horror and torment! I do not remember every single detail but will try to share it with you to the best of my abilities.

Everything started like I was in some kind of dream but still it was real. A very bright figure accompanied by two angels approached me. At first I did not know who that Person was, but after that I understood it was Jesus. He said: "Yoel, I want to show you something." Then I saw two clouds in front of us: a cloud of light and a cloud of darkness. Jesus and the angels took me through the dark cloud. Then we went through what seemed to be the gates of hell (Mathew 16:18). Suddenly, I saw a hallway with a large line of people who had shackles on their legs. They were lining up to what seemed to be a torture chamber. Inside the chamber I saw two huge demons that were torturing the people. They were tearing the limbs away from their bodies. The pain, screams and horror were greater than anybody could bear.

After that I saw people burning in fire. The strangest thing was that the fire was burning without making any light. Also, I saw some kind of reptiles eating through the skin of the people (Mark 9:43-48). Their pain was unimaginable. Some of the faces I saw belonged to people I had previously known.

Then we walked down another hallway. At the end of it, I saw a throne and the ugliest creature I had ever seen was sitting on it. At first I thought it was Satan, but after my experience was over, I thought more about it and cannot definitely say if it was him or some lead demon.

That was the end of my tour. Jesus and the angels took me, we went through the cloud of light this time, and I was back in my body.

# How to Enter
# Into the Kingdom?

## Nicodemus' Perspective

*It was one of those starry nights in the Middle East when the sky looked so low you could almost touch it. In the shadows of the night, a man wearing a big turban and clothes indicating social prominence was making his way through the dark streets. The man was a little nervous and was trying to avoid the few people who were outside at that late hour. He was bothered by that uneasy feeling on the inside. Having studied and taught the oracles of Yahweh for years, he was still looking for answers. He knew that something was missing. For the last few days, he had been listening to that strange Rabbi from Galilee, and every time he would hear His sayings about the Kingdom of God or see the miracles, an unknown mix of hope, fear and religious pride would rise in his heart.*

*Finally, the man arrived at the door of the house where that teacher who called himself Messiah was staying. While lifting his hand to knock on the door, the fear of being humiliated pierced his stomach again. He was ready to go back. But then…Then he would not have the answers, the truth about the Kingdom of Jehovah, The One who he so greatly loved and feared. He knocked on the door….*

**Val:** This is a presumptive story of how one of the most prominent Jewish teachers of his day came to Jesus to find the missing answers about Him and the Kingdom of Heaven. I would call it the Nicodemus's Perspective. An authentic account of what happened after he arrived at the house where Jesus stayed can be found in the Gospel of John, 3:1-7.

*"There was a man from of the Pharisees named Nicodemus, a ruler of the Jews. This man came to Jesus by night and said to Him: "Rabbi, we know that You are a teacher come from God; for no one can do these signs that You do unless God is with him."*

*Jesus answered and said to him, "Most assuredly, I say to you, unless one is born again, he cannot see the Kingdom of God." Nicodemus said to Him, "How can a man be born when he is old? Can he enter a second time into his mother's womb and be born?" Jesus answered: "Most assuredly I say to you, unless one is born of water and the Spirit he cannot enter the kingdom of God. That which is born of the flesh is flesh, and that which is born of the Spirit is spirit. Do not marvel that I said to you, "You must be born again"*
(emphasis added).

Maybe you have the same fears or uncertainty that the fictional Nicodemus I created had. Probably you have tried religion in some form and still have not received the answers you seek. Or chances are, you have already realized the reality of the Kingdom but have the same question the real Nicodemus had: how to enter into and be part of it?

The answer is the same one that he got: <u>you must be born again</u>! You must repent of your sin, ask God to forgive you and receive the atonement of Jesus as a personal gift. He died for your sins, was buried and on the third day rose from the dead for your justification.The Bible, which is the constitution of the Kingdom, says:

*"…if you confess with your mouth the Lord Jesus and believe in your heart that God has raised Him from the dead, you will be saved. For with the heart one believes unto righteousness, and with the mouth confession is made unto salvation. For the Scripture says, "Whoever believes on Him will not be put to shame." For there is no distinction between Jew and Greek, for the same Lord over all is rich to all who call upon Him. For "whoever calls on the name of the Lord shall be saved."*

(Romans 10:9-13)

To make it easier for you I have included a simple prayer with which you can approach God, The King of Heaven and Earth (please pray even if you once have known the Lord but have backslidden. He has never stopped loving you):

*"God, I come to you in the name of Jesus. I repent of my sins and ask for Your forgiveness. Cleanse me with the blood of Jesus. Come into my heart and renew it. I believe that Jesus died for my sin and was raised from the dead for my forgiveness and justification. I confess Him as the Lord of my life and completely surrender myself to Him. Please fill me with your Holy Spirit. Thank you."*

If you have prayed sincerely and in faith this prayer, you are born again into the Kingdom of God. Congratulations! The King is now your Father. You can approach Him at any time with any question or concern you may have. He is more than willing to listen to your prayers and to answer them. God the Father loves you as much as He loves His Son, Jesus Christ.

The next step you should take is to find a good Bible-believing church and become a part of it. Ask to be baptized in water as an outward expression of your inward decision to follow Jesus Christ. Get a copy of the Bible and read it every day, preferably starting with the Gospel of John. Forsake any evil acts and communications. May God bless you!

# Final words

We want to thank you for the time you have shared with us reading this book. We do not take the investment of your precious time lightly. It has been a privilege to share our stories and testimonies with you. Our prayer is that,

If you were without Jesus, now you are born again into His Kingdom;

If you were a backslider from the faith, now you are in the arms of the Father again;

If you were in torment of evil, now hope and deliverance have shone for you;

If you were stagnant in your walk with the Lord, now you have been provoked to more radical commitment.

Please let us know if this book has blessed your life. We will be glad to pray for any of your needs and answer any of your questions.

And remember:

**His Kingdom is at hand!**

# About the Authors

**Val Kanchelov** graduated from the Law School of St. Kliment Ohridski University of Sofia, Bulgaria. During his study, he accepted Jesus Christ as his Lord and Savior and has served Him in different capacities for more than 16 years. In 2001, Val and his family moved to the United States where he later became the founder of Messengers of Righteousness Ministry International located in Atlanta, Georgia. Val has appeared on TV shows such as *Atlanta Live* with Betty Cornett and *Changing Your World* with Creflo Dollar. God confirms his ministry with the healing and delivering power of the Holy Spirit. Val is also a realtor licensed with the state of Georgia.

**Mariya Kanchelov** was called to a prophetic ministry as a student in communist Bulgaria when God took her to Heaven and revealed her assignment. In the 1990s, she was a part of a team that planted a number of churches throughout Bulgaria. She also served as a Bible School teacher and a conference speaker. After her marriage to Val, she submitted her gifts and talents to help her husband. Mariya's preaching of the Word is accompanied by mighty manifestations of the gifts of the Holy Spirit.

Val and Mariya have two children, Yoel and Raphael.